NOCTURNE

Thank you, Moses Znaimer,
for a lifetime (well, almost...)
of inspiration and support.

For backing me in everything I wanted to do,
whatever form it might take
(and there've been a few...)

Thank you.

Thank you, my love.

—M.L.

All paintings featured in the book are by Marilyn Lightstone.

www.plumleafpress.com

Every reasonable effort has been made to trace the owners of copyrighted material and to make due acknowledgement. Any errors or omissions drawn to our attention will be gladly rectified in future editions.

23 24 25 26 27   5 4 3 2 1

ISBN 978-1-7388982-0-6

Printed in China

NOCTURNE

Poems to Linger Over

POEMS SELECTED BY

Marilyn Lightstone

CONTENTS

MEETING AT NIGHT

I ASK MY MOTHER TO SING

AFTERNOON ON A HILL

SO WE'LL GO NO MORE A ROVING

FOREWORD

These poems are food for the soul.

In her own inimitable way, Marilyn has chosen poems that reflect her philosophy, and her elegant taste and style.

From Emily Dickinson to Leonard Cohen, Robert Browning to Michael Ondaatje, Maya Angelou to Paul Verlaine, to name just a few of the famous ones, we are given the chance to read, to reflect, and to savour these stirring words that cause us to ponder the meaning of life in so many ways. And when Marilyn reads them with her sensual velvety voice, the words come alive perfectly.

Here is a poem that hit home for me, as I have just completed a painting of me swimming.

THE AVOWAL
Denise Levertov

As swimmers dare
to lie face to the sky
and water bears them,
as hawks rest upon air
and air sustains them,
so would I learn to attain
freefall, and float
into Creator Spirit's deep embrace,
knowing no effort earns
that all-surrounding grace.

So, a piece of visual poetry seemed appropriate to accompany these magic words in the NOCTURNE collection. It's truly inspirational.

Thank you, Marilyn!

— *Charles Pachter*

GLIDE, acrylic on canvas, 2023, by Charles Pachter

INTRODUCTION

"And 'What (you may ask) is a poem to an actress like yourself?'
And I would reply, 'Why, a mini drama, of course!'"

How extraordinary that the beautiful, tragic, inspiring, and amusing thoughts, feelings, and experiences of someone who may have lived long ago and far away, or who may be alive now, someone whom we have never met or had the opportunity to meet, should be available to us in such glorious profusion; a lifetime of wit or wisdom available at any time of the day or night to everyone — whatever their place in the hierarchy of age, experience, or fortune. Happiness and heartbreak, expressed in a stanza that takes as long to read as sipping a cup of tea or drinking a glass of water.

Such is poetry ...

The poems in this book were gathered lovingly from many, many sources, including the Internet. They were married to a classical music radio show on The New Classical FM — and not incidentally, dear reader — *Nocturne* — a name now shared by the beautiful volume you hold in your hand.

> **"Happiness and heartbreak, expressed in a stanza that takes as long to read as sipping a cup of tea or drinking a glass of water."**

Poets and their poems ...

As many as I could find to please a loyal and enthusiastic audience that — to my delight and endless gratitude — embraced them with enthusiasm and joy. Indeed, most of the mail I receive is about the poetry!

And here we are. Yet another journey this motley crew of words is making in time and in the world ...

Oh! And I want you to know ...

Holding this book in my hand fills me with me the greatest of joy. The poems herein have created a beautiful on-air community for me, and let me tell you: poetry lovers are Very Nice People.

We LOVE this book! (And we hope you will, too.)

But enough: you want to get reading ...

— Marilyn Lightstone

THE MUSE

THE MUSE
Anna Akhmatova

When at night I await her coming,
life, it seems, hangs by a thread.
That honours, that youth, that freedom fade
before my dear guest with flute in hand.

And here she comes. Throwing back her veil,
intently she looks at me.
I ask: "Did you dictate to Dante
the pages of his Inferno?" She answers: "I did."

LINES LOST AMONG THE TREES
Billy Collins

These are not the lines that came to me
while walking in the woods
with no pen
and nothing to write on anyway.

They are gone forever,
a handful of coins
dropped through the grate of memory,
along with the ingenious mnemonic

I devised to hold them in place —
all gone and forgotten
before I had returned to the clearing of lawn
in back of our quiet house

with its jars jammed with pens,
its notebooks and reams of blank paper,
its desk and soft lamp,
its table and the light from its windows.

So this is my elegy for them,
those six or eight exhalations,
the braided rope of syntax,
the jazz of the timing,

and the little insight at the end
wagging like the short tail
of a perfectly obedient spaniel
sitting by the door.

This is my envoy to nothing
where I say Go, little poem —
not out into the world of strangers' eyes,
but off to some airy limbo,

home to lost epics,
unremembered names,
and fugitive dreams
such as the one I had last night,

which, like a fantastic city in pencil,
erased itself
in the bright morning air
just as I was waking up.

SPRING NIGHT
Sara Teasdale

The park is filled with night and fog,
The veils are drawn about the world,
The drowsy lights along the paths
Are dim and pearled.

Gold and gleaming the empty streets,
gold and gleaming the misty lake,
The mirrored lights like sunken swords,
Glimmer and shake.

Oh, is it not enough to be
Here with this beauty over me?
My throat should ache with praise, and I
Should kneel in joy beneath the sky.
O, Beauty, are you not enough?
Why am I crying after love,
With youth, a singing voice and eyes
To take earth's wonder with surprise?
Why have I put off my pride,
Why am I unsatisfied,—
I, for whom the pensive night
Binds her cloudy hair with light,—
I, for whom all beauty burns
Like incense in a million urns?
O, Beauty, are you not enough?
Why am I crying after love?

LETTERS
Bozor Sobir

I opened your letters
And I gave them up to the air,
That they might become spring clouds.
That letters of memories
Might weep over the hills,
That they might weep springs and rivers.
That the letters might weep over us.
Last night I told a story
Of you to the wild wind.
In memory of you I recited from memory
A verse to the streams,
That the water might bear it away
And tell it to the rivers,
That the wind might bear it away
And sing it to the plains.
Last night under the rain
I walked road by road in my thoughts.
Your tresses strand by strand,
In my thoughts I walked, braiding strands.
The kisses that had not been planted on your lips

— Along, all along the road,
Along the edge, the edge of the stream —
I walked, planting them in the ground.
So that, ever following in my footsteps
— Along, all along the road,
On the edge, the edge of the stream —
Kisses might grow like daisies,
Kisses might grow like wild mint.
Last night it rained and rained.
The water was too much for the river to hold.
Last night my loneliness
Was too much for me alone to hold . . .
Last night the April rain
Washed the footprints from the ground.
The wound in my heart grew worse,
Because it washed away the imprint of your foot.
Last night I wandered the streets in vain,
Like a hunter who has lost the trail I searched . . .
Last night the world was all water,
The sky was refreshed,
The ground was refreshed.
But I, with your name on my lips,
All alone like the parched land
I burned up under the rain.

THIS IS A LOVE POEM WITHOUT RESTRAINT
Lorna Crozier

This poem
is full of pain
full of pieces
It cries out
oh! oh! oh!
It has no pride
no discretion
It whimpers
It will not drop its eyes
when it meets a stranger
It will not hide
its tears

It will talk
of beauty
Lilacs Apples
The smell of rain
in caraganas
Your mouth
your eyes

What are you going to do about it?
You cannot stop me
now

•

The moon shines on this page
as the poem writes
itself. It is trying to find
whiteness
frost on snow

two feathers
on a pillow
your hands
      upon
my skin

•

These words are tired
of being
      words
They refuse to sit here
pretending
      they can't move
            off the page

These are the first
ones to leave
their white space
They fall
on your tongue
letter
          by
                letter
like raindrops

One of them
is my name

What will you do with it?
It has decided to live
inside you
.
This poem has no restraint
It will not say
plum blossom
sunset
rubbing stone
cat's cradle

It refuses to be evasive

I miss you
I miss you
Come home

•

It won't talk of passion
but the sleep that follows
when our bodies
touch

that moment
just before waking
when we realize
we've been holding one another
in our sleep

•

How do you use the word love
in a poem?

Love.

If you look at it
long enough
it will burn into your eyes

JOY
Lisel Mueller

"Don't cry, its only music,"
someone's voice is saying.
"No one you love is dying."
It's only music. And it was only spring,
the world's unreasoning body
run amok, like a saint's, with glory,
that overwhelmed a young girl
into unreasoning sadness.
"Crazy," she told herself,
"I should be dancing with happiness."
But it happened again. It happens
when we make bottomless love —
there follows a bottomless sadness
which is not despair
but its nameless opposite.
It has nothing to do with the passing of time.
It's not about loss. It's about
two seemingly parallel lines
suddenly coming together
inside us, in some place
that is still wilderness.
Joy, joy, the sopranos sing,
reaching for the shimmering notes
while our eyes fill with tears.

MARTHA GRAHAM
James Laughlin

Earth and water air
and fire; her body

Beats the ground. It
flows; it floats; it

Seems to burn. She
burns herself away

Until there is no
body there at all

But only the pure
elements moving as

Music moves moving
from her into us

I HAVE NOT LINGERED IN EUROPEAN MONASTERIES
Leonard Cohen

I have not lingered in European monasteries
and discovered among the tall grasses tombs of knights
who fell as beautifully as their ballads tell;
I have not parted the grasses
or purposefully left them thatched.

I have not released my mind to wander and wait
in those great distances
between the snowy mountains and the fishermen,
like a moon,
or a shell beneath the moving water.
I have not held my breath
so that I might hear the breathing of God,
or tamed my heartbeat with an exercise,
or starved for visions.

Although I have watched him often
I have not become the heron,
leaving my body on the shore,
and I have not become the luminous trout,
leaving my body in the air.

I have not worshipped wounds and relics,
or combs of iron,
or bodies wrapped and burnt in scrolls.

I have not been unhappy for ten thousand years.
During the day I laugh and during the night I sleep.
My favourite cooks prepare my meals,
my body cleans and repairs itself,
and all my work goes well.

"HOPE" IS THE THING WITH FEATHERS
Emily Dickinson

"Hope" is the thing with feathers —
That perches in the soul —
And sings the tune without the words —
And never stops — at all —

And sweetest — in the Gale — is heard —
And sore must be the storm —
That could abash the little Bird
That kept so many warm —

I've heard it in the chillest land —
And on the strangest Sea —
Yet, never, in Extremity,
It asked a crumb — of me.

THE AVOWAL
Denise Levertov

As swimmers dare
to lie face to the sky
and water bears them,
as hawks rest upon air
and air sustains them,
so would I learn to attain
freefall, and float
into Creator Spirit's deep embrace,
knowing no effort earns
that all-surrounding grace.

MEETING

AT

NIGHT

MEETING AT NIGHT
Robert Browning

I

The grey sea and the long black land;
And the yellow half-moon large and low;
And the startled little waves that leap
In fiery ringlets from their sleep,
As I gain the cove with pushing prow,
And quench its speed i' the slushy sand.

II

Then a mile of warm sea-scented beach;
Three fields to cross till a farm appears;
A tap at the pane, the quick sharp scratch
And blue spurt of a lighted match,
And a voice less loud, thro' its joys and fears,
Than the two hearts beating each to each!

PERFUME
Hanjo Takehara

perfume ...
that night, that time
that place ...

RAINY COTTAGE
Ikuyo Yoshimura

rainy cottage ...
after lovemaking
the scent of jasmine tea ...

NIGHTS OF SPRING
Yoshiko Yoshino

nights of spring ...
tides swelling within me
as I'm embraced ...

THE CINNAMON PEELER
Michael Ondaatje

If I were a cinnamon peeler
I would ride your bed
and leave the yellow bark dust
on your pillow.

Your breasts and shoulders would reek
you could never walk through markets
without the profession of my fingers
floating over you. The blind would
stumble certain of whom they approached
though you might bathe
under rain gutters, monsoon.

Here on the upper thigh
at this smooth pasture
neighbour to your hair
or the crease
that cuts your back. This ankle.
You will be known among strangers
as the cinnamon peeler's wife.

I could hardly glance at you
before marriage
never touch you
—your keen nosed mother, your rough brothers.
I buried my hands
in saffron, disguised them
over smoking tar,
helped the honey gatherers ...

When we swam once
I touched you in the water
and our bodies remained free,

you could hold me and be blind of smell.
you climbed the bank and said

this is how you touch other women
the grass cutter's wife, the lime burner's daughter.
And you searched your arms
for the missing perfume

and knew

what good is it
to be the lime burner's daughter
left with no trace
as if not spoken to in the act of love
as if wounded without the pleasure of a scar.

You touched
your belly to my hands
in the dry air and said
I am the cinnamon
peeler's wife. Smell me.

THANK YOU, MY FATE
Anna Swir

Great humility fills me,
great purity fills me,
I make love with my dear
as if I made love dying
as if I made love praying,
tears pour
over my arms and his arms.
I don't know whether this is joy
or sadness, I don't understand
what I feel, I'm crying,
I'm crying, it's humility
as if I were dead,
gratitude, I thank you, my fate,
I'm unworthy, how beautiful
my life.

GOOD GOD, WHAT A NIGHT THAT WAS
Petronius Arbiter

Good God, what a night that was,
The bed was so soft, and how we clung,
Burning together, lying this way and that,
Our uncontrollable passions
Flowing through our mouths.
If only I could die that way,
I'd say goodbye to the business of living.

BENDS
Erín Moure

When the heart is not enough.
That I can open it &
let you enter
an ocean so dense
you'll get the bends if you surface.
That you will be open to the love of every being:
I crave this, it makes me possible, anarchic, calling
your attention,
your fingers' madness on my ear or soft neck,
the light on each side of your face, altered
as you speak to me

Oh speak to me
I have a friend who says the heart's
a shovel, do you believe this?
My heart is a wild muscle, that's all,
open as the ocean
at the end of the railway,
a cross-country line pulled by four engines
whatever it is I don't care, it is not enough
unless you see it
unless I make you embrace & breathe in it,
its light that knows you,
unless you cry out in it, & swim

SONNETS FROM THE PORTUGUESE XIV
Elizabeth Barrett Browning

If thou must love me, let it be for nought
Except for love's sake only. Do not say
'I love her for her smile —her look —her way
Of speaking gently, —for a trick of thought
That falls in well with mine, and certes brought
A sense of pleasant ease on such a day' —
For these things in themselves, Beloved, may
Be changed, or change for thee, —and love, so wrought,
May be unwrought so. Neither love me for
Thine own dear pity's wiping my cheeks dry, —
A creature might forget to weep, who bore
Thy comfort long, and lose thy love thereby!
But love me for love's sake, that evermore
Thou mayst love on, through love's eternity.

THE EXQUISITE HOUR
Paul Verlaine

The moon white
Glows in the woods;
From each sprout
Comes forth a voice
Below the arbors …

O my precious.

The pond does reflect,
Profound mirror,
The silhouette
Of a black willow
Where wind does whimper …

Let us dream! It is the hour.

A vast and fond
Calmness
Seems to descend
From the heavens
Which the orb lets iridescent …

It is the hour exquisite.

THE ENDURING QUALITY OF LOVE
Lady Horikawa

How can one e'er be sure
If true love will endure?
My thoughts this morning are
as tangled as my hair.

TO THE TUNE OF "ATTACHED TO HER SKIRT"
Madame Wei

The lamp flickers bright, bright, and the water clock drips and drips.

Now that my lover has left

the night is so cold.

A frenzied west wind blows and fetches me back from dream.

Does anyone miss me

as I lean alone on my pillow

with knitted brows?

My brocade screen and embroidered drapes show in autumn dawn.

This pain breaks me inside

and I shed secret tears.

I still see a bright moon in my small west window.

I hate you,

I adore you,

but what would you know of that?

FROM THE BEGINNING
Fujiwara no Teika

From the beginning
I knew meeting could only
end in parting, yet
I ignored the coming dawn
and I gave myself to you.

AS SWEET
Wendy Cope

It's all because we're so alike —
Twin souls, we two.
We smile at the expression, yes,
And know it's true.
I told the shrink.
He gave our love
A different name.
But he can call it what he likes —
It's still the same.
I long to see you, hear your voice,
My narcissistic object-choice.

I ASK
MY MOTHER
TO SING

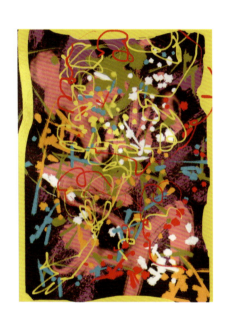

I ASK MY MOTHER TO SING
Li-Young Lee

She begins, and my grandmother joins her.
Mother and daughter sing like young girls.
If my father were alive, he would play
his accordion and sway like a boat.

I've never been in Peking, or the Summer Palace,
nor stood on the great Stone Boat to watch
the rain begin on Kuen Ming Lake, the picnickers
running away in the grass.

But I love to hear it sung;
how the waterlilies fill with rain until
they overturn, spilling water into water,
then rock back, and fill with more.

Both women have begun to cry.
But neither stops her song.

IT IS MARVELLOUS TO WAKE UP TOGETHER
Elizabeth Bishop

It is marvellous to wake up together
At the same minute; marvellous to hear
The rain begin suddenly all over the roof,
To feel the air suddenly clear
As if electricity had passed through it
From a black mesh of wires in the sky.
All over the roof the rain hisses,
And below, the light falling of kisses.

An electrical storm is coming or moving away;
It is the prickling air that wakes us up.
If lighting struck the house now, it would run
From the four blue china balls on top
Down the roof and down the rods all around us,
And we imagine dreamily
How the whole house caught in a bird-cage of lightning
Would be quite delightful rather than frightening;

And from the same simplified point of view
Of night and lying flat on one's back
All things might change equally easily,
Since always to warn us there must be these black
Electrical wires dangling. Without surprise
The world might change to something quite different,
As the air changes or the lightning comes without our blinking,
Change as our kisses are changing without our thinking.

THE EBONY CHICKERING

Dorianne Laux

My mother cooked with lard she kept
in coffee cans beneath the kitchen sink.
Bean-colored linoleum ticked under her flats
as she wore a path from stove to countertop.
Eggs cracked against the lips of smooth
ceramic bowls she beat muffins in,
boxed cakes and cookie dough.
It was the afternoons she worked toward,
the smell of onions scrubbed from her hands,
when she would fold her flowered apron
and feed it through the sticky refrigerator
handle, adjust the spongy curlers on her head
and wrap a loud Hawaiian scarf into a tired knot
around them as she walked toward her piano,
the one thing my father had given her that she loved.
I can still see each gold letter engraved
on the polished lid she lifted and slid
into the piano's dark body, the hidden hammers
trembling like a muffled word,
the scribbled sheets, her rough hands poised
above the keys as she began her daily practice.
Words like *arpeggio* sparkled through my childhood,
her fingers sliding from the black bar of a sharp
to the white of a common note. "This is Bach,"
she would instruct us, the tale of his name hissing
like a cat. "And Chopin," she said, "was French,
like us," pointing to the sheet music. "Listen.

Don't let the letters fool you. It's best
to always trust your ear."
She played parts of fugues and lost concertos,
played hard as we kicked each other on the couch,
while the meat burned and the wet wash wrinkled
in the basket, played Beethoven as if she understood
the caged world of the deaf, his terrible music
pounding its way through the fence slats
and the screened doors of the cul-de-sac, the yards
where other mothers hung clothes on a wire, bent
to weeds, swept the driveways clean.
Those were the years she taught us how to make
quick easy meals, accept the embarrassment
of a messy house, safety pins and rick-rack
changing from the hem of her dress.
But I knew the other kids didn't own words
like *fortissimo* and *mordant, treble clef*
and *trill*, or have a mother quite as elegant
as mine when she sat at her piano,
playing like she was famous,
so that when the Sparklets man arrived
to fill our water cooler every week
he would lean against the doorjamb and wait
for her to finish, glossy-eyed
as he listened, secretly touching the tips
of his fingers to the tips of her fingers
as he bowed, and she slipped him the check.

THE PROS AND CONS
Sophie Hannah

He'll be pleased if I phone to ask him how he is.
It will make me look considerate and he likes considerate people.

He'll be reassured to see that I haven't lost interest,
Which might make him happy and then I'll have done him a favour.

If I phone him right now I'll get to speak to him sooner
Than I will if I sit around waiting for him to phone me.

He might not want to phone me from work in case someone hears
And begins (or continues) to suspect that there's something
Between us.

If I want to and don't, aren't I being a bit immature?
We're both adults. Does it matter, with adults, who makes the
First move?

But there's always the chance he'll back off if I come on too strong.
The less keen I appear, the more keen he's likely to be,

And I phoned him twice on Thursday and once on Friday.
He must therefore be fully aware that it's his turn, not mine.

If I make it too easy for him, he'll assume I'm too easy,
While if I make no effort, that leaves him with more of a challenge.

I should demonstrate that I have a sense of proportion.
His work must come first for a while and I shouldn't mind waiting.

For all I know he could have gone off me already
And if I don't phone I can always say, later, that I went off him first.

WHEN A WOMAN LOVES A MAN
David Lehman

When she says margarita she means daiquiri.
When she says *quixotic* she means *mercurial.*
And when she says, "I'll never speak to you again,"
she means, "Put your arms around me from behind
as I stand disconsolate at the window."

He's supposed to know that.

When a man loves a woman he is in New York and she is in Virginia
or he is in Boston, writing, and she is in New York, reading,
or she is wearing a sweater and sunglasses in Balboa Park and he
        is raking leaves in Ithaca
or he is driving to East Hampton and she is standing disconsolate
        at the window overlooking the bay
where a regatta of many-colored sails is going on
while he is stuck in traffic on the Long Island Expressway.

When a woman loves a man it is one ten in the morning
she is asleep he is watching the ball scores and eating pretzels
drinking lemonade
and two hours later he wakes up and staggers into bed
where she remains asleep and very warm.

When she says tomorrow she means in three or four weeks.
When she says, "We're talking about me now,"
he stops talking. Her best friend comes over and says,
"Did somebody die?"

When a woman loves a man, they have gone
to swim naked in the stream
on a glorious July day
with the sound of the waterfall like a chuckle
of water rushing over smooth rocks,
and there is nothing alien in the universe …

FLOWERS IN THE KITCHEN
Lemn Sissay

On buying her flowers
she said

"There's no food in the kitchen
and we can't eat flowers."

On buying her food
she said

"You don't buy flowers any more."

HAIKU
Hyakuchi

With one who does not
speak his every thought
I spent a pleasant evening ...

HAIKU
Taniko Terai

A man reading
A woman sleeping ...
the snowy sky ...

ALONE
Maya Angelou

Lying, thinking
Last night
How to find my soul a home
Where water is not thirsty
And bread loaf is not stone
I came up with one thing
And I don't believe I'm wrong
That nobody,
But nobody
Can make it out here alone.

Alone, all alone
Nobody, but nobody
Can make it out here alone.

There are some millionaires
With money they can't use
Their wives run round like banshees
Their children sing the blues
They've got expensive doctors
To cure their hearts of stone.
But nobody
No, nobody
Can make it out here alone.

Alone, all alone
Nobody, but nobody
Can make it out here alone.

Now if you listen closely
I'll tell you what I know
Storm clouds are gathering
The wind is gonna blow
The race of man is suffering
And I can hear the moan,
'Cause nobody,
But nobody
Can make it out here alone.

Alone, all alone
Nobody, but nobody
Can make it out here alone.

DESTINY
Edwin Arnold

Somewhere there waiteth in this world of ours
For one lone soul another lonely soul
Each choosing each through all the weary hours
And meeting strangely at one sudden goal.
Then blend they, like green leaves with golden flowers,
Into one beautiful and perfect whole;
And life's long night is ended, and the way
Lies open onward to eternal day.

SHAKE HANDS
A. E. Housman

Shake hands, we shall never be friends, all's over;
I only vex you the more I try.
All's wrong that ever I've done or said,
And nought to help it in this dull head:
Shake hands, here's luck, good-bye.

But if you come to a road where danger
Or guilt or anguish or shame's to share,
Be good to the lad that loves you true
And the soul that was born to die for you,
And whistle and I'll be there.

AFTERNOON ON A HILL

AFTERNOON ON A HILL
Edna St. Vincent Millay

I will be the gladdest thing
  Under the sun!
I will touch a hundred flowers
  And not pick one.

I will look at cliffs and clouds
  With quiet eyes,
Watch the wind bow down the grass,
  And the grass rise.

And when lights begin to show
  Up from the town,
I will mark which must be mine,
  And then start down!

ANTHEM
Leonard Cohen

The birds they sang
At the break of day
Start again
I heard them say
Don't dwell on what has passed away
Or what is yet to be
Ah, the wars they will be fought again
The holy dove, she will be caught again
Bought and sold, and bought again
The dove is never free
Ring the bells that still can ring
Forget your perfect offering
There is a crack, a crack in everything
That's how the light gets in
We asked for signs
The signs were sent
The birth betrayed
The marriage spent
Yeah, and the widowhood
Of every government
Signs for all to see
I can't run no more
With that lawless crowd
While the killers in high places
Say their prayers out loud

But they've summoned, they've summoned up
A thundercloud
They're going to hear from me
Ring the bells that still can ring
Forget your perfect offering
There is a crack, a crack in everything
That's how the light gets in
You can add up the parts
But you won't have the sum
You can strike up the march
There is no drum
Every heart, every heart
To love will come
But like a refugee
Ring the bells that still can ring
Forget your perfect offering
There is a crack, a crack in everything
That's how the light gets in
Ring the bells that still can ring
Forget your perfect offering
There is a crack, a crack in everything
That's how the light gets in
That's how the light gets in
That's how the light gets in

THE WAKING
Theodore Roethke

I wake to sleep, and take my waking slow.
I feel my fate in what I cannot fear.
I learn by going where I have to go.

We think by feeling. What is there to know?
I hear my being dance from ear to ear.
I wake to sleep, and take my waking slow.

Of those so close beside me, which are you?
God bless the Ground! I shall walk softly there,
And learn by going where I have to go.

Light takes the Tree; but who can tell us how?
The lowly worm climbs up a winding stair;
I wake to sleep, and take my waking slow.

Great Nature has another thing to do
To you and me; so take the lively air,
And, lovely, learn by going where to go.

This shaking keeps me steady. I should know.
What falls away is always. And is near.
I wake to sleep, and take my waking slow.
I learn by going where I have to go.

SOMETHING
Kimiko Hahn

Resting her on my chest like a sleeping cat
I cannot recall my older daughter so small and new
and fear the memory of this
complete, absolute something will grow away
and fear the hand will never remember
stroking her head as she nursed
or fear I'll forget her soft cry
when I look up from sleep and see you lift her
4 am, the curtains blowing in and out of the window
as the whole house breathes.

YOU DO NOT NEED MANY THINGS
Taigu Ryokan

My house is buried in the deepest recess of the forest
Every year, ivy vines grow longer than the year before.
Undisturbed by the affairs of the world I live at ease,
Woodmen's singing rarely reaching me through the trees.
While the sun stays in the sky, I mend my torn clothes
And facing the moon, I read holy texts aloud to myself.
Let me drop a word of advice for believers of my faith.
To enjoy life's immensity, you do not need many things.

MIND WANTING MORE
Holly J. Hughes

Only a beige slat of sun
above the horizon, like a shade

pulled not quite down. Otherwise,
clouds. Sea rippled here and
there. Birds reluctant to fly.

The mind wants a shaft of sun to
stir the grey porridge of clouds,
an osprey to stitch sea to sky
with its barred wings, some dramatic
music: a symphony, perhaps

a Chinese gong.
But the mind always
wants more than it has—
one more bright day of sun,
one more clear night in bed
with the moon; one more hour
to get the words right; one
more chance for the heart in hiding
to emerge from its thicket
in dried grasses—as if this quiet day
with its tentative light weren't enough,
as if joy weren't strewn all around.

ROOFS
Joyce Kilmer

The road is wide and the stars are out
And the breath of the night is sweet,
And this is the time when wanderlust should seize upon my feet.
But I'm glad to turn from the open road and the starlight on my face,
And to leave the splendour of out-of-doors for a human dwelling place.

I never have seen a vagabond who really liked to roam
All up and down the streets of the world and not to have a home:
The tramp who slept in your barn last night and left at break of day
Will wander only until he finds another place to stay.

A gypsy-man will sleep in his cart with canvas overhead;
Or else he'll go into his tent when it is time for bed.
He'll sit on the grass and take his ease so long as the sun is high,
But when it is dark he wants a roof to keep away the sky.

If you call a gypsy a vagabond, I think you do him wrong,
For he never goes a-travelling but he takes his home along.
And the only reason a road is good, as every wanderer knows,
Is just because of the homes, the homes, the homes to which it goes.

They say that life is a highway and its milestones are the years,
And now and then there's a toll-gate where you buy your way with tears.
It's a rough road and a steep road and it stretches broad and far,
But at last it leads to a golden Town where golden Houses are.

UP-HILL
Christina Rossetti

Does the road wind up-hill all the way?
  Yes, to the very end.
Will the day's journey take the whole long day?
  From morn to night, my friend.

But is there for the night a resting-place?
  A roof for when the slow dark hours begin.
May not the darkness hide it from my face?
  You cannot miss that inn.

Shall I meet other wayfarers at night?
  Those who have gone before.
Then must I knock, or call when just in sight?
  They will not keep you standing at that door.

Shall I find comfort, travel-sore and weak?
  Of labour you shall find the sum.
Will there be beds for me and all who seek?
  Yea, beds for all who come.

DOG-TIRED

D.H. Lawrence

If she would come to me here
Now the sunken swaths
Are glittering paths
To the sun, and the swallows cut clear
Into the setting sun! if she came to me here!

If she would come to me now,
Before the last-mown harebells are dead;
While that vetch-clump still burns red!
Before all the bats have dropped from the bough
To cool in the night; if she came to me now!

The horses are untackled, the chattering machine
Is still at last. If she would come
We could gather up the dry hay from
The hill-brow, and lie quite still, till the green
Sky ceased to quiver, and lost its active sheen.

I should like to drop
On the hay, with my head on her knee,
And lie dead still, while she
Breathed quiet above me; and the crop
Of stars grew silently.

I should like to lie still
As if I was dead; but feeling
Her hand go stealing
Over my face and my head, until
This ache was shed.

FERN HILL
Dylan Thomas

Now as I was young and easy under the apple boughs
About the lilting house and happy as the grass was green,
    The night above the dingle starry,
      Time let me hail and climb
    Golden in the heydays of his eyes,
And honoured among wagons I was prince of the apple towns
And once below a time I lordly had the trees and leaves
    Trail with daisies and barley
Down the rivers of the windfall light.

And as I was green and carefree, famous among the barns
About the happy yard and singing as the farm was home,
    In the sun that is young once only,
      Time let me play and be
    Golden in the mercy of his means,
And green and golden I was huntsman and herdsman, the calves
Sang to my horn, the foxes on the hills barked clear and cold,
    And the sabbath rang slowly
    In the pebbles of the holy streams.

All the sun long it was running, it was lovely, the hay
Fields high as the house, the tunes from the chimneys, it was air
    And playing, lovely and watery
      And fire green as grass.
    And nightly under the simple stars
As I rode to sleep the owls were bearing the farm away,
All the moon long I heard, blessed among stables, the nightjars
    Flying with the ricks, and the horses
      Flashing into the dark.

And then to awake, and the farm, like a wanderer white
With the dew, come back, the cock on his shoulder: it was all
   Shining, it was Adam and maiden,
     The sky gathered again
   And the sun grew round that very day.
So it must have been after the birth of the simple light
In the first, spinning place, the spellbound horses walking warm
   Out of the whinnying green stable
     On to the fields of praise.

And honoured among foxes and pheasants by the gay house
Under the new made clouds and happy as the heart was long,
   In the sun born over and over,
     I ran my heedless ways,
   My wishes raced through the house high hay
And nothing I cared, at my sky blue trades, that time allows
In all his tuneful turning so few and such morning songs
   Before the children green and golden
     Follow him out of grace,

Nothing I cared, in the lamb white days, that time would take me
Up to the swallow thronged loft by the shadow of my hand,
   In the moon that is always rising,
     Nor that riding to sleep
   I should hear him fly with the high fields
And wake to the farm forever fled from the childless land.
Oh as I was young and easy in the mercy of his means,
     Time held me green and dying
   Though I sang in my chains like the sea.

THE BAGEL
David Ignatow

I stopped to pick up the bagel
rolling away in the wind,
annoyed with myself
for having dropped it
as if it were a portent.
Faster and faster it rolled,
with me running after it
bent low, gritting my teeth,
and I found myself doubled over
and rolling down the street
head over heels, one complete somersault
after another like a bagel
and strangely happy with myself.

SONG FOR A BLUE ROADSTER
Rachel Field

Fly, Roadster, fly!
The sun is high,
Gold are the fields
We hurry by,
Green are the woods
As we slide through
Past harbor and headland,
Blue on blue.

Fly, Roadster, fly!
The hay smells sweet,
And the flowers are fringing
Each village street,
Where carts are blue
And barns are red,
And the road unwinds
Like a twist of thread.

Fly, Roadster, fly!
Leave Time behind;
Out of sight Shall be out of mind.
Shine and shadow
Blue sea, green bough,
Nothing is real
But Here and Now.

SO WE'LL

GO NO MORE

A ROVING

SO WE'LL GO NO MORE A ROVING
George Gordon, Lord Byron

So, we'll go no more a roving
    So late into the night,
Though the heart be still as loving,
    And the moon be still as bright.

For the sword outwears its sheath,
    And the soul wears out the breast,
And the heart must pause to breathe,
    And love itself have rest.

Though the night was made for loving,
    And the day returns too soon,
Yet we'll go no more a roving
    By the light of the moon.

ODE 44
Hafez

Last night, as half asleep I dreaming lay,
Half naked came she in her little shift,
With tilted glass, and verses on her lips;
Narcissus-eyes all shining for the fray,
Filled full of frolic to her wine-red lips,
Warm as a dewy rose, sudden she slips
Into my bed – just in her little shift.

Said she, half naked, half asleep, half heard,
With a soft sigh betwixt each lazy word,
 'Oh my old lover, do you sleep or wake!'
And instant I sat upright for her sake,
And drank whatever wine she poured for me –
Wine of the tavern, or vintage it might be
Of Heaven's own vine: he surely were a churl
Who refused wine poured out by such a girl,
A double traitor he to wine and love.

Go to, thou puritan! the gods above
Ordained this wine for us, but not for thee;
Drunkards we are by a divine decree,
Yea, by the special privilege of heaven
Foredoomed to drink and foreordained forgiven.

Ah! HAFIZ, you are not the only man
Who promised penitence and broke down after;
For who can keep so hard a promise, man,
With wine and woman brimming o'er with laughter!
O knotted locks, filled like a flower with scent,
How have you ravished this poor penitent!

THE HUG
Thom Gunn

It was your birthday, we had drunk and dined
　　Half of the night with our old friend
　　　Who'd showed us in the end
　　To a bed I reached in one drunk stride.
　　　Already I lay snug,
And drowsy with the wine dozed on one side.

I dozed, I slept. My sleep broke on a hug,
　　　Suddenly, from behind,
In which the full lengths of our bodies pressed:
　　　Your instep to my heel,
　　My shoulder-blades against your chest.
　　It was not sex, but I could feel
　　The whole strength of your body set,
　　　Or braced, to mine,
　　　And locking me to you
　　As if we were still twenty-two
　　When our grand passion had not yet
　　　Become familial.
　　My quick sleep had deleted all
　　Of intervening time and place.
　　　I only knew
The stay of your secure firm dry embrace.

FRIENDSHIP AFTER LOVE
Ella Wheeler Wilcox

After the fierce midsummer all ablaze
Has burned itself to ashes, and expires
In the intensity of its own fires,
There come the mellow, mild, St. Martin days
Crowned with the calm of peace, but sad with haze.
So after Love has led us, till he tires
Of his own throes, and torments, and desires,
Comes large-eyed friendship: with a restful gaze,
He beckons us to follow, and across
Cool verdant vales we wander free from care.
Is it a touch of frost lies in the air?
Why are we haunted with a sense of loss?
We do not wish the pain back, or the heat;
and yet, and yet, these days are incomplete.

THE LONGLY-WEDS KNOW
Leah Furnas

That it isn't about the Golden Anniversary at all,
But about all the unremarkable years
that Hallmark doesn't even make a card for.

It's about the 2nd anniversary when they were surprised to
find they cared for each other more than last year

And the 4th when both kids had chickenpox
and she threw her shoe at him for no real reason

And the 6th when he accidentally got drunk on the way
home from work because being a husband and father
was so damn hard

It's about the 11th and 12th and 13th years when
they discovered they could survive crisis

And the 22nd anniversary when they looked
at each other across the empty nest, and found it good.

It's about the 37th year when she finally
decided she could never change him

And the 38th when he decided
a little change wasn't that bad

It's about the 46th anniversary when they both
bought cards, and forgot to give them to each other
But most of all it's about the end of the 49th year
when they discovered you don't have to be old

to have your 50th anniversary!!!!

WHEN YOU ARE OLD
W. B. Yeats

When you are old and grey and full of sleep,
And nodding by the fire, take down this book,
And slowly read, and dream of the soft look
Your eyes had once, and of their shadows deep;

How many loved your moments of glad grace,
And loved your beauty with love false or true,
But one man loved the pilgrim soul in you,
And loved the sorrows of your changing face;

And bending down beside the glowing bars,
Murmur, a little sadly, how Love fled
And paced upon the mountains overhead
And hid his face amid a crowd of stars.

THE LAST ROSE OF SUMMER
Thomas Moore

Tis the last rose of Summer,
  Left blooming alone;
All her lovely companions
  Are faded and gone;
No flower of her kindred,
  No rose-bud is nigh,
To reflect back her blushes
  Or give sigh for sigh!

I'll not leave thee, thou lone one,
  To pine on the stem;
Since the lovely are sleeping,
  Go sleep thou with them.
Thus kindly I scatter
  Thy leaves o'er the bed
Where thy mates of the garden
  Lie scentless and dead.

So soon may I follow,
  When friendships decay,
And from Love's shining circle
  The gems drop away!
When true hearts lie withered,
  And fond ones are flown,
Oh! who would inhabit
  This bleak world alone?

OLD MAN EATING ALONE IN A CHINESE RESTAURANT
Billy Collins

I am glad I resisted the temptation,
if it was a temptation when I was young,
to write a poem about an old man
eating alone at a corner table in a Chinese restaurant.

I would have gotten it all wrong
thinking: the poor bastard, not a friend in the world
and with only a book for a companion.
He'll probably pay the bill out of a change purse.

So glad I waited all these decades
to record how hot and sour the hot and sour
soup is here at Chang's this afternoon
and how cold the Chinese beer in a frosted glass.

And my book—José Saramago's *Blindness*
as it turns out—is so absorbing that I look up
from its escalating horrors only
when I am stunned by one of his gleaming sentences.

And I should mention the light
that falls through the big windows this time of day
italicizing everything it touches—
the plates and teapots, the immaculate tablecloths,

as well as the soft brown hair of the waitress
in the white blouse and short black skirt,
the one who is smiling now as she bears a cup of rice
and shredded beef with garlic to my favorite table in the corner.

ULYSSES

Alfred, Lord Tennyson

It little profits that an idle king,
By this still hearth, among these barren crags,
Match'd with an aged wife, I mete and dole
Unequal laws unto a savage race,
That hoard, and sleep, and feed, and know not me.
I cannot rest from travel: I will drink
Life to the lees: All times I have enjoy'd
Greatly, have suffer'd greatly, both with those
That loved me, and alone, on shore, and when
Thro' scudding drifts the rainy Hyades
Vext the dim sea: I am become a name;
For always roaming with a hungry heart
Much have I seen and known; cities of men
And manners, climates, councils, governments,
Myself not least, but honour'd of them all;
And drunk delight of battle with my peers,
Far on the ringing plains of windy Troy.

I am a part of all that I have met;
Yet all experience is an arch wherethro'
Gleams that untravell'd world whose margin fades
For ever and forever when I move.
How dull it is to pause, to make an end,
To rust unburnish'd, not to shine in use!
As tho' to breathe were life! Life piled on life
Were all too little, and of one to me
Little remains: but every hour is saved
From that eternal silence, something more,
A bringer of new things; and vile it were
For some three suns to store and hoard myself,
And this gray spirit yearning in desire
To follow knowledge like a sinking star,
Beyond the utmost bound of human thought …

There lies the port; the vessel puffs her sail:
There gloom the dark, broad seas. My mariners,
Souls that have toil'd, and wrought, and thought with me —
That ever with a frolic welcome took
The thunder and the sunshine, and opposed
Free hearts, free foreheads — you and I are old;
Old age hath yet his honour and his toil;
Death closes all: but something ere the end,
Some work of noble note, may yet be done,
Not unbecoming men that strove with Gods.
The lights begin to twinkle from the rocks:
The long day wanes: the slow moon climbs: the deep
Moans round with many voices. Come, my friends,
'T is not too late to seek a newer world.
Push off, and sitting well in order smite
The sounding furrows; for my purpose holds
To sail beyond the sunset, and the baths
Of all the western stars, until I die.
It may be that the gulfs will wash us down:
It may be we shall touch the Happy Isles,
And see the great Achilles, whom we knew.
Tho' much is taken, much abides; and tho'
We are not now that strength which in old days
Moved earth and heaven, that which we are, we are;
One equal temper of heroic hearts,
Made weak by time and fate, but strong in will
To strive, to seek, to find, and not to yield.

DO NOT GO GENTLE INTO THAT GOOD NIGHT
Dylan Thomas

Do not go gentle into that good night,
Old age should burn and rave at close of day;
Rage, rage against the dying of the light.

Though wise men at their end know dark is right,
Because their words had forked no lightning they
Do not go gentle into that good night.

Good men, the last wave by, crying how bright
Their frail deeds might have danced in a green bay,
Rage, rage against the dying of the light.

Wild men who caught and sang the sun in flight,
And learn, too late, they grieved it on its way,
Do not go gentle into that good night.

Grave men, near death, who see with blinding sight
Blind eyes could blaze like meteors and be gay,
Rage, rage against the dying of the light.

And you, my father, there on the sad height,
Curse, bless, me now with your fierce tears, I pray.
Do not go gentle into that good night.
Rage, rage against the dying of the light.

LOVELIEST OF TREES
A.E. Housman

Loveliest of trees, the cherry now
Is hung with bloom along the bough,
And stands about the woodland ride
Wearing white for Eastertide.
Now, of my threescore years and ten,
Twenty will not come again,
And take from seventy springs a score,
It only leaves me fifty more.
And since to look at things in bloom
Fifty springs are little room,
About the woodlands I will go
To see the cherry hung with snow.

LONG LIFE
Elaine Feinstein

Late Summer. Sunshine. The eucalyptus tree.
    It is a fortune beyond any deserving
to be still *here*, with no more than everyday worries,
    placidly arranging lines of poetry.

I consider a stick of cinammon
    bound in raffia, finches
in the grass, and a stubby bush
    which this year mothered a lemon.

These days I speak less of death
    than the mysteries of survival. I am
no longer lonely, not yet frail, and
    after surgery, recognise each breath

as a miracle. My generation may not be
    nimble but, forgive us,
we'd like to hold on, stubbornly
    content — even while ageing.

IF I CAN STOP ONE HEART FROM BREAKING
Emily Dickinson

If I can stop one heart from breaking,
I shall not live in vain;

If I can ease one life the aching,
Or cool one pain,
Or help one fainting robin
Unto his nest again,
I shall not live in vain.

"I want to be thoroughly used up when I die, for the harder I work, the more I live. I rejoice in life for its own sake. Life is no 'brief candle' to me. It is sort of a splendid torch which I have a hold of for the moment, and I want to make it burn as brightly as possible before handing it over to future generations."

— *George Bernard Shaw*

About Marilyn Lightstone

Just as the poetry and paintings in *Nocturne: Poems to Linger Over*, nourish her soul, so too do Marilyn Lightstone's many other ongoing and meaningful projects. On television, she produces and hosts VisionTV's *Your All-Time Classic Hit Parade*, now going into its sixth season, and she continues to be known in countries around the world as the beloved Miss Muriel Stacy in the classic *Anne of Green Gables*. She's the signature voice of ZoomerMedia's VisionTV and The New Classical FM, as well as *Marilyn Lightstone Reads*, the audiobook podcast (with over a half a million downloads to date) inspired by her love of reading classic literature aloud. Musically speaking, Marilyn's original compositions include a reinterpretation of "In Flanders Fields," the Thanksgiving song "Blessings," and her interfaith Christmas/Chanukah carol "The Light Shines All Over the World."

This veteran of stage and screen recalls her most memorable performances as Leah in *The Dybbuk;* as Mary in *Mary, Queen of Scots* at the Charlottetown Festival; and as part of the New York and Los Angeles casts of the interactive theatrical phenomenon *Tamara*. She equally cherishes being cast in seminal Canadian films such as *Lies My Father*

Told Me, In Praise of Older Women, and *The Tin Flute,* for which she received the Best Actress Award from the Moscow International Film Festival, presented by the world's first female cosmonaut, Valentina Tereshkova. Marilyn's novel, *Rogues and Vagabonds,* was inspired by her life as an actress.

Described as a "force of nature" by *Zoomer* magazine, simply put, Marilyn is one of Canada's most cherished and multi-faceted artists. Most recently, she was honoured by the 30th annual Toronto Jewish Film Festival for her outstanding and prolific artistic career and rich contribution to Canadian culture.

Thank you from Marilyn ...

Rebecca Bender and Jen Harvey, the designers who are responsible for the beauty of the book, and the cover.

As well as ...
I'm over the moon with the cover photo!

Stellar photographer, my lovely friend Yuri Dojc (who never leaves home without a camera in his pocket) snapped it on a bright, hot, summer day (and I tweaked it about; just a little ...).

Siobhan Grennan is yet another star in my firmament, who, among her many virtues, had the stamina and patience to comb through hundreds of episodes, separating the poems from the gorgeous music we play seven days a week.

And then, of course, there's Leanne Wright, ZoomerMedia's "Minister of Propaganda" who, with the lightest and most loving touch, makes wonderful things happen.

All, however, acknowledge — as I do — that the driving force behind *Nocturne: Poems to Linger Over* is the extraordinary, indefatigable Maggie Goh, the President and Publisher of Plumleaf Press. I flatter myself by saying that all of her books are polished and elegant, and poetry seems to emanate from her very pores.